Elegant Appetizers

A Collection of Recipes with International Flair

Elegant Appetizers

A Collection of Recipes with International Flair

Betty Evans

Gulf Publishing Company
Houston, Texas

Elegant Appetizers

A Collection of Recipes with International Flair

Gulf Publishing Company
Book Division
P.O. Box 2608 • Houston, Texas 77252-2608

10 9 8 7 6 5 4 3 2 1

Library of Congress Cataloging-in-Publication Data

Evans, Betty.
  Elegant appetizers : a collection of recipes with international
flair / Betty Evans.
     p.   cm.
  Includes index.
  ISBN 0-88415-591-9 (alk. paper)
  1. Appetizers.   2. Cookery, International.   I. Title.
TX740.E82   1998
641.8′12—dc21   98-24791
                                                               CIP

Printed in Hong Kong

Photography by Mary Herrmann
Food styling by Lee Stanyer
Cover design by Laura Dion
Book design by Roxann L. Combs

Dedication

For Gordon, who is forever my favorite and dearest dining companion.

Contents

Acknowledgments

Thanks to my three children, Bob, Suzanne, and Jeanne, who always have been enthusiastic about every food I have ever cooked. Together we have shared dining and cooking experiences in many kitchens around the world, backyard gardens, and camping tables under the pines. With their vivacious spirit, they have made these adventures fun and memorable. All of these special memories were an inspiration to me in writing this book.

Special thanks to Steve Hoffmann for always bright and amazing computer help, discerning proofreading, and extravagant sharing of his time.

To my late friend M.F.K. Fisher, who always stressed the best things in food only need to be uncomplicated and honest.

My thanks to my Gulf editor, Kelly Perkins, for her discriminating and careful editing of this book.

Lastly I hope that my grandchildren, Gordon, Evelyn, Zachary, and Alex, will always be able in their lives to have the joy of sharing food together.

Introduction

Versatile, Wonderful Appetizers!

Appetizers can act as the prelude to the main meal, or they may accompany liquid refreshments for festive parties and special occasions. People can enjoy appetizers while standing up or sitting down. Some appetizers may be nibbled over a napkin, while others should be served on small plates to catch any crumbs or drips. Little forks are handy if needed. For a large crowd, appetizers can be passed or set out on a table.

This versatile way of entertaining is well-suited for celebrations, fund-raisers, open houses, receptions, showers, weddings, holidays, pre-game parties, picnics, and graduations. The menu choices should fit the mood of the event, and the preparation and planning should be a chance for anyone to engage in pleasurable creativity.

The origins of the custom of serving appetizers are ancient because the need is so basic. Humans have always wanted a little social moment to relax and anticipate dining. Early Greeks served cheeses, olives, marinated octopus, and shrimp. They called this *orektika*, which means "a provocative to drinking." The Romans named their appetizers *gustatio*. Popular selections for them included oysters, spicy sausages, fried snails, and seasoned lentils. In Russia, diverse appetizers were spread on a large table covered with a white linen tablecloth. This presentation of appetizers, named *zakusi*, was intended to help absorb the serious vodka drinking. The French adopted this custom from the Russians in the nineteenth century, calling their version *hors d'oeuvre a la russe* ("before the main work, Russian style"). The French also describe appetizers with the fanciful term *amuse bouche,* which translates as "amusements for the mouth." In today's Italy, appetizers are *antipasto* ("before the pasta"). The Germans' *vorspiesen* translates as "before the food." Hot cheese pastries and sausages are popular for this. Bars in Spain are spread with little plates of myriad tempting tiny foods titled *tapas,* which are served with sherry or wine. Scandinavians present a *smörgåsbord,* a table filled with varied fish preparations and exquisite tiny sandwiches. Sliced, hot, crisp egg rolls and piquant, little ribs are part of the Chinese menu. Every region of our world offers its own distinct contribution. In America we have our own special appetizers, which show a rich variety of worldwide influences created with our own Yankee ingenuity.

To aid in the preparation and serving of the appetizers in this cookbook, here are a few general guidelines. It is difficult to exactly determine the precise amount of servings that each recipe in this book will provide. I have attempted to provide a practicable number. The determining factor will depend on the occasion and appetites of the guests. A general rule for serving is no more than three appetizers before dinner. However, if the situation is a party or reception and the only food is appetizers, you will need more. Try to offer a nice variety of both hot and cold. You will find the recipes in this book are categorized as hot/warm and cold/cool to assist with your preparation. Also, I have experimented with freezing various appetizers, and convenient as this procedure may be, the result is not very good. Most appetizers can be prepared ahead and easily kept refrigerated.

There is a special joy associated with creating appetizers, perhaps because sharing food and drink with others is always one of life's pleasures.

Betty Evans

Hermosa Beach, Calif.

Classic Dips & Spreads

Quick Blue Cheese & Celery Spread, p. 10

France

Betty Wynn's Chicken Liver Pâté

Over the years I have tasted and made numerous kinds of chicken liver appetizers, and this one from Betty Wynn one of my best friends, is still my favorite. It has the perfect flavor combination, the preparation is simple, and it has an impressive appearance.

¼ POUND (4 OUNCES) SWEET BUTTER (BUTTER WITHOUT ADDED SALT)

1 SMALL WHITE ONION, CHOPPED

1 CLOVE GARLIC, MINCED

1 POUND CHICKEN LIVERS, VERY FRESH

SALT AND PEPPER TO TASTE

1 (10- TO 12-OUNCE) CAN CHICKEN OR BEEF CONSOMMÉ

¼ CUP WHITE WINE OR BRANDY

1 (8-OUNCE) PACKAGE CREAM CHEESE

1 (4-OUNCE) PACKAGE BLUE CHEESE

1 ENVELOPE KNOX GELATIN, DISSOLVED IN ¼ CUP HOT WATER

2 TABLESPOONS TRUFFLES (A UNIQUE ROOT DELICACY) OR BLACK OLIVES
FOR GARNISH (CANNED IS FINE)

WATERCRESS FOR GARNISH

To keep sweet butter fresh, store in your freezer. Remove cubes as needed.

Melt the butter in a frying pan. Gently fry the onion and garlic just until limp. Add chicken livers to the pan, and fry until livers are slightly pink inside. Sprinkle with salt and pepper to taste. Add 4 teaspoons of the consommé, reserving the rest of the can for later. Add the wine or brandy. Cool slightly. Add the cheeses. Place the mixture in a blender and blend until smooth. Set aside in a cool place until you are ready to place the blended chicken liver mixture on top of the aspic, which is simply a

COLD/COOL

mixture of dried gelatin and consommé with a thick jelly consistency.

To Prepare the Aspic

Heat the remainder of the consommé. Dissolve gelatin in ¼ cup hot water as per package directions, and add to the consommé. Pour into a 3- to 4-cup mold or a stainless steel bowl. Refrigerate until slightly thick (about 10 minutes). Remove from refrigerator and make your own desired design with the olives or truffles. They may be cut in slices, rings, squares, or triangles to create a simple design. Simply place them on top of the aspic carefully. It's fun to make a little creation on the aspic. Return to refrigerator for 20 minutes to set.

To Prepare for Serving

Remove aspic from refrigerator and carefully place the chicken liver mixture on the aspic. Chill overnight. To unmold, set the pan in warm water. When slightly loose around the edges, turn out onto a platter. Refrigerate until needed.

This will keep for 2 to 3 days, covered with plastic or foil wrap.

To serve, garnish with watercress and serve with rye bread rounds or crackers. If you are in a hurry, forget the aspic, and simply place the pâté in pretty bowls 2 to 3 inches deep. Provide a wide-edged knife or tablespoon for serving. The pâté is served as a slice (not always perfect) with the aspic included. You may unmold the pâté and pre-cut it in about ⅓-inch slices, but people do enjoy taking their own portion from this tempting pâté.

Serves 8.

When purchasing watercress, be sure you select a bunch that is all bright green without yellowing leaves. The unique, peppery flavor makes watercress a popular, piquant appetizer garnish.

Mexico

Cilantro, sometimes called Chinese parsley, is grown from the coriander seed. The plant and the seed have two distinctly different flavors.

To keep cilantro fresh and perky, place stems in a glass jar filled with water (like a bouquet). The leaves should be just above the jar rim. Loosely cover the leaves with plastic, and keep refrigerated. Cut leaves as you need them.

COLD/COOL

Fiesta Taco Tart

These taco tarts have the ideal blend of Mexican-influenced flavors. You can easily make them ahead and avoid last-minute fuss.

1   (17-OUNCE) CAN REFRIED BEANS
1   (8-OUNCE) CARTON SOUR CREAM
1   (1¼-OUNCE) PACKAGE TACO SEASONING
1   MEDIUM AVOCADO, MASHED AND LIGHTLY SALTED (OR 1 [8-OUNCE] CAN
      GUACAMOLE)
1   CUP SALSA
2   GREEN ONIONS, CHOPPED FINE
2   CUPS CHEDDAR OR MONTEREY JACK CHEESE, GRATED
1   (2.2-OUNCE) CAN CHOPPED OLIVES
2   MEDIUM TOMATOES, DICED
    CILANTRO FOR GARNISH
    STURDY CORN OR TORTILLA CHIPS FOR DIPPING

In a 10- or 12-inch pie pan or bowl, spread out the beans. Smooth the top. Spread the sour cream over the beans. Sprinkle half the taco seasoning on the sour cream, and reserve the other half.

Spread the avocado or guacamole over the taco seasoning, followed by the salsa. Sprinkle the onions over the salsa. Next, scatter the cheese over the onions. Add remaining half of taco seasoning over the cheese. Now sprinkle the olives over the seasoning, followed by the tomatoes. Cover and refrigerate an hour or so for flavors to mellow. Garnish with cilantro. Serve with a sturdy chip that can dip down through the layers without crumbling apart.

Serves 6 to 8.

California Guacamole

California

Avocado groves are part of the California landscape, even though the tree is a native of Mexico. Records show that the Mayans enjoyed avocados as far back as 300 B.C. Franciscan padres planted the seeds in California mission gardens.

Guacamole is simply lightly mashed avocados with seasonings. It is best made fresh or else the special light-green color will turn brown in spite of any tricks you may try.

2   RIPE AVOCADOS, PITTED AND PEELED
1   RIPE MEDIUM-SIZED UNPEELED TOMATO, CUT IN TINY PIECES
2   GREEN ONIONS, MINCED
1   TEASPOON CHILI POWDER
1   TABLESPOON LIME JUICE OR LEMON JUICE
     SALT AND PEPPER TO TASTE
1   CLOVE GARLIC, PEELED AND FINELY MINCED
1   SMALL ANAHEIM OR JALAPEÑO PEPPER, FINELY MINCED (OPTIONAL)
1   TABLESPOON FRESH SNIPPED CILANTRO LEAVES (OPTIONAL)

Coarsely mash the avocados with a fork in a bowl (around 3-cup size). Leave some tiny lumps for texture. Never use a blender or processor for guacamole, as it will make a mushy puree, which is not desirable. Gently mix in remaining ingredients. Serve immediately with carnitas (see recipe on page 73) or tortilla chips.

Serves 6 to 8.

The best varieties of avocados for making guacamole are Haas and Fuerte. Sometimes the avocado is called an alligator pear because it is shaped like a pear and, with a little imagination, the skin has a texture similar to alligator skin.

COLD/COOL

Bangkok,
Thailand

Bangkok Avocado Dip

The piquant flavors of Thailand combine wonderfully well with avocado to make a spirited appetizer. This combination brings out all the flavorful qualities of the fruit.

2   RIPE AVOCADOS, PEELED

2   TABLESPOONS LIME JUICE

1   TABLESPOON FRESH CILANTRO, MINCED

1   RED PEPPER, DICED FINE (1 CUP BOTTLED OR CANNED)

½   MEDIUM RED ONION, FINELY CHOPPED

  SALT AND PEPPER TO TASTE

  DASH OF HOT SAUCE OR TABASCO

Make this appetizer just before serving for the best color and freshest flavor.

Cut the avocados in half, and remove seeds. Use a fork to mash avocados to a medium lumpy texture. Fold in remaining ingredients, mix well, and place in a medium-sized bowl.

Shrimp chips (*kroe poeck*), found in Asian grocery stores, are the traditional accompaniment. However, sturdy potato chips work as well.

Serves 6 to 8.

COLD/COOL

Holiday Olive Spread or Dip

United States

If during the holiday season you are invited to a party and want to prepare something ahead of time that you can just snatch out of the refrigerator on your way to the festivities, this recipe is ideal. The olives add distinctive flavor to the cream cheese and butter mixture.

⅛ POUND UNSALTED BUTTER

1 MEDIUM ONION, FINELY CHOPPED

1 (8-OUNCE) PACKAGE CREAM CHEESE, ROOM TEMPERATURE

1 (8-OUNCE) CAN GREEN OR BLACK PITTED OLIVES

½ TEASPOON CHILI POWDER

  CILANTRO SPRIGS, DICED RED PEPPER, AND/OR DICED PARSLEY FOR
  GARNISH (OPTIONAL)

Melt the butter in a small frying pan. Add the onion, and cook just until soft and limp. You do not want the onion browned. Cool slightly.

Place the cream cheese in a medium-sized bowl. Add the butter-onion mixture, and cream together with an electric mixer or by hand.

Drain and coarsely chop the olives. Mix the olives and chili powder into the creamed mixture by hand or with an electric mixer. Place in one bowl, or several small bowls, and chill.

This may be kept in the refrigerator for up to a week.

To serve, garnish with fresh cilantro if desired. If used at Christmas, finely chopped red pepper and parsley make a nice garnish. Serve as a spread with crackers or sturdy tortilla chips. Also, celery and carrot sticks may be used for dipping.

This will serve 6 to 8.

This appetizer may be presented in one large bowl or several small bowls.

COLD/COOL

7

Provence Tapenade

In the olive-growing region of Provence, this piquant black-olive mixture is popular as a spread for bread and as a dip for the area's lovely vegetables.

1   (2-OUNCE) CAN ANCHOVY FILETS

¾ CUP GREEK OR NIÇOISE OLIVES, PITTED

¼ CUP CAPERS

¼ CUP OLIVE OIL

1   CLOVE GARLIC, CHOPPED

1   TEASPOON BLACK PEPPER

Remove anchovies from can, place in a strainer, and set strainer in the sink. Run cold water over anchovies to rinse away the excess salt. Drain, and transfer to a medium-sized bowl. Mix in remaining ingredients.

Put mixture in a blender, and turn the blender on and off quickly until the mixture is coarsely chopped (you want to keep a slight texture). Scrape down the insides of the blender during the process. This mixture was originally made with a mortar and pestle, which is still a perfectly good method if you care to do it that way.

This will keep, refrigerated, for 2 to 3 weeks.

In Avignon, France, tapenade is often served with slices of sturdy brown bread or toast. It also makes a nice topping for hard-boiled egg halves.

Serves 4 to 5.

Sans une bonne table, il n'y a pas de plaisir."*Without a good table, there is no pleasure" is a traditional expression from this sun-drenched region of France.*

COLD/COOL

Hummus

 Turkey

This healthy and satisfying dip is an indispensable part of Middle Eastern cuisine. When I was on a tour of Turkey, our group frequently ate buffet dinners. This gave everyone the opportunity to sample the country's famous cuisine. A large bowl of hummus was always on the table, surrounded with freshly baked pita bread.

1   (15- OR 16-OUNCE) CAN GARBANZO BEANS (CHICK-PEAS)

2   CLOVES GARLIC, PEELED AND CHOPPED

¼   CUP FRESH LEMON JUICE (SQUEEZED FROM 2 MEDIUM LEMONS)

1   TEASPOON SALT OR TO TASTE

2   TABLESPOONS SESAME OIL

FRESH SNIPPED PARSLEY (OR MINT) AND PAPRIKA FOR GARNISH

Drain the chick-peas, reserving 1 tablespoon of the liquid. Place chick-peas, 1 tablespoon reserved liquid, garlic, lemon juice, salt, and sesame oil in blender. Blend until smooth.

Serve in a bowl garnished with parsley and paprika. Pita bread cut in triangles is the traditional accompaniment. Hummus can be kept in the refrigerator up to a week.

This will serve 8.

This food has been used for centuries, especially in the Mediterranean region. Records show chick-peas grew in the famed Hanging Gardens of Babylon.

COLD/COOL

United States

Buy celery with green and fresh-looking leaves. The leaves can be finely snipped and used as a pretty garnish. For peak freshness, wrap celery in damp paper towels and store refrigerated in a plastic bag.

Quick Blue Cheese & Celery Spread

Quite often you may need a quick and easy appetizer at the last minute. This flavorful spread is speedily prepared and always popular with guests.

½ CUP BLUE CHEESE, ROOM TEMPERATURE

½ CUP CREAM CHEESE, ROOM TEMPERATURE

3 TABLESPOONS FRESH CELERY, FINELY CHOPPED

FRESHLY GROUND PEPPER TO TASTE

Combine all the ingredients in a medium-sized bowl. Blend together thoroughly with a spoon or fork. Chill until serving time, and serve with crackers of your choice. Any that is left over can serve as a tasty topping for baked potatoes. This spread can be kept a week in the refrigerator.

This will serve 4.

COLD/COOL

Hungarian Liptauer Spread

Hungary

This delectable mixture of flavors from Hungary is internationally popular as an appetizer and is easily prepared ahead. In Budapest restaurants, a pretty, glazed pottery bowl filled with the spread is placed on your table. These restaurants serve the spread with rye toast.

¼ CUP SWEET BUTTER (BUTTER WITHOUT ADDED SALT), ROOM TEMPERATURE

8 OUNCES CREAM CHEESE, ROOM TEMPERATURE

1 TABLESPOON CAPERS, MINCED

1 TABLESPOON CARAWAY SEED

3 TABLESPOONS CHIVES OR GREEN ONION TOPS, MINCED

1 TABLESPOON DIJON-STYLE MUSTARD

1 TABLESPOON PAPRIKA

¼ TEASPOON SALT

¼ CUP SOUR CREAM

½ TEASPOON ANCHOVY PASTE OR 2 MINCED ANCHOVIES (OPTIONAL)

A tube of anchovy paste kept in your refrigerator is always handy for a little extra dash of flavor in foods and salad dressings.

Cream the butter and cream cheese together. This may be done by hand in a medium-sized bowl by using a wooden spoon or in an electric mixer. Add remaining ingredients and blend with mixer or spoon. Place in desired size bowls, cover, and refrigerate. This will keep in the refrigerator for up to a week.

Before serving, let stand at room temperature for 20 minutes for easier spreading. Serve with thinly sliced dark bread, toast, or crackers.

Serves 6.

COLD/COOL

From front to back:
Potted Shrimp,
Potted Cheddar Cheese &
Green Onion, and Potted
Ham & Cheese.

Potted Appetizers

This classic style of appetizer has some distinct advantages. It may be prepared ahead, allowing the flavors to mellow and blend, which results in a most savory taste. These tasty mixtures, served in attractive pots or crocks, are always tempting.

Potted Shrimp

1 POUND BAY (OR OTHER TINY) SHRIMP, COOKED AND DEVEINED

½ CUP SWEET BUTTER (BUTTER WITHOUT ADDED SALT)

   SALT AND PEPPER TO TASTE

⅛ TEASPOON NUTMEG

In a medium-sized bowl, mash the shrimp slightly with a fork, retaining a texture. Set aside. In a medium-sized saucepan, melt the butter with the seasonings. Remove from the stove, add shrimp, and mix. Pack into a crockery jar or little bowl. Place in refrigerator until needed; this will keep for several days. Serve with toast or crackers.

This will serve 6 to 8.

Potted Cheddar Cheese & Green Onion

1 POUND SHARP CHEDDAR, GRATED, ROOM TEMPERATURE

3 TABLESPOONS GREEN ONION, MINCED

1 TEASPOON DIJON OR ENGLISH COLEMAN'S MUSTARD

2 TABLESPOONS SHERRY

   DASH OF WORCESTERSHIRE OR TABASCO SAUCE

Cream all ingredients until smooth. This may be done in a medium-sized bowl with a wooden spoon or electric mixer. Pack into bowl or crock. Serve at room temperature for easier spreading, with crusty bread slices, toast, or crackers. This may be kept a week refrigerated.

This will serve 8.

 *Great Britain*

Potted shrimp is a traditional British appetizer. This pale pink creation is delicate, pretty, and refreshing and has been served since the time of the Tudors.

COLD/COOL

 *Great Britain*

Potted Ham & Cheese

¾ CUP COOKED HAM, MINCED

1 CUP SHARP CHEDDAR CHEESE, GRATED

2 GREEN ONIONS, MINCED

2 TABLESPOONS CAPERS

1 TABLESPOON DIJON MUSTARD

¾ CUP MAYONNAISE

2 TABLESPOONS SHERRY

¼ TEASPOON GRATED NUTMEG

   SALT AND PEPPER TO TASTE

Combine all ingredients in a medium-sized bowl. Blend together until smooth, either by hand with a wooden spoon or by using an electric mixer or food processor. Pack into bowl or crock and refrigerate up to a week. Serve with rye crackers.

This will serve 6 to 8.

See Potted Ham & Cheese photo, p. 12.

Potted Cheddar Cheese

8 OUNCES SHARP CHEDDAR CHEESE, GRATED

2 OUNCES BUTTER, ROOM TEMPERATURE

   PINCH NUTMEG

2 TABLESPOONS WHITE WINE OR SHERRY

In a medium-sized bowl, mix all ingredients together with a fork or spoon until well blended and creamy. Pack into crocks or little bowls. Refrigerated, this will keep well for up to a week.

Remove from refrigerator 30 minutes before serving, for easier spreading. Serve with toast, crackers, or celery sticks.

This will serve 8.

COLD/COOL

New Mexico Chile con Queso

New Mexico

Chile con queso (melted cheese with green chiles) is the perfect chilly-weather appetizer. While traditionally served with tortilla chips, it also makes a nice dip for vegetables or breadsticks. This basic chile con queso can be fancied up by adding, at the final stage, a cup of fresh crabmeat, cooked bay shrimp, or cooked and drained chorizo (spicy Mexican sausage).

2 TABLESPOONS BUTTER OR VEGETABLE OIL

1 LARGE ONION, FINELY CHOPPED (ABOUT 1 CUP)

1 CLOVE GARLIC, MINCED

1 (28-OUNCE) CAN WHOLE TOMATOES, DRAINED

2 (7-OUNCE) CANS DICED GREEN CHILES, DRAINED

SALT TO TASTE

¼ TEASPOON GROUND CUMIN (OPTIONAL)

1 OR 2 FINELY CHOPPED JALAPEÑO PEPPERS FOR ADDED HEAT (OPTIONAL)

½ POUND SHARP CHEDDAR CHEESE (OR MONTEREY JACK), GRATED

Melt the butter (or heat the vegetable oil) on the stove in a heavy pot (1½-quart size). A heavy pot will regulate the heat so the cheese will melt nicely. Add onion and garlic, and sauté over low heat, stirring until the onions are limp and translucent but not browned. While the onion and garlic are cooking, finely chop the drained tomatoes and chiles. Season with salt and cumin. Add tomatoes and chiles to onion mixture, and cook 15 minutes over a low flame, stirring occasionally, until the mixture is slightly thick. Add jalapeños if used. Blend in the cheese and any additional ingredients of your choice. Stir just until cheese is melted. Do not let this boil, as the cheese will become tough.

Serve while warm. This may be kept hot with a heat tray or candle warmer. Sometimes chile con queso is spooned over tortilla chips on individual plates.

This will serve 6.

Beer is a popular beverage with chile con queso. Arrange assorted, chilled bottled beer on a tray, with beer glasses and a bottle opener, for guests to select their favorite brew.

HOT/WARM

Castroville,
California

Castroville Hot Artichoke Dip

The small town of Castroville, in northern California, is located in the heart of the state's prime artichoke lands. The cool, green fields stretch for miles. Along the roadside are rustic stands with fresh artichokes for sale and modest little cafés that feature dishes created from artichokes. One of the most popular is this hot dip.

1 (10-OUNCE) PACKAGE FROZEN ARTICHOKE HEARTS OR 1 (14-OUNCE) CAN
   ARTICHOKE HEARTS

1 (10-OUNCE) PACKAGE FROZEN CHOPPED SPINACH, COOKED, OR 1 BUNCH
   FRESH SPINACH, COOKED, DRAINED, AND CHOPPED (ABOUT 1 CUP)

½ CUP MAYONNAISE

1 CUP PARMESAN CHEESE, GRATED

2 FINELY CHOPPED WHOLE GREEN ONIONS OR 2 TABLESPOONS FINELY
   CHOPPED WHITE ONIONS

1 CLOVE GARLIC, PEELED AND MINCED

SALT AND PEPPER TO TASTE

1 TEASPOON BUTTER OR OLIVE OIL FOR BAKING DISH

If you have difficulty chopping the hearts, try using a pair of kitchen scissors for this task.

If using frozen artichoke hearts, cook them as per package instructions and drain. If using canned, drain. Finely chop or mash the hearts in a medium-sized bowl. Mix with the remaining ingredients except the butter or olive oil. Lightly butter or oil a 1½-quart baking dish and transfer mixture from bowl to baking dish. Bake at 350° for 15 to 20 minutes, uncovered. The mixture should be hot and bubbly. Serve hot with crackers or chips.

This serves 4 to 6.

HOT/WARM

Southwest Bean Dip

New Mexico

In our American Southwest, bean dips are always a popular part of the appetizer menu. This recipe is simple and well-flavored.

1   (16-OUNCE) CAN REFRIED BEANS

1   (2¼-OUNCE) CAN CHOPPED BLACK OLIVES, DRAINED

1   MEDIUM WHITE ONION, FINELY CHOPPED

1   CLOVE GARLIC, PEELED AND MINCED

1   CUP MONTEREY JACK OR CHEDDAR CHEESE, GRATED

½   CUP SALSA

1   OR 2 FINELY DICED JALAPEÑO CHILES FOR ADDITIONAL HEAT (OPTIONAL)

Combine all ingredients in a baking dish (quart-sized or close). Bake uncovered at 350° for 30 minutes. Serve with large, sturdy tortilla chips.

This dip may be prepared ahead and kept refrigerated until time for baking; just bake about 10 extra minutes if cold.

This will serve 6 to 8.

If you use a heavy baking dish, the dip will stay warm for the party. You may also place the dish on a heating tray to keep the dip warm.

HOT/WARM

Sumptuous

Fruit

&

Vegetable

Appetizers

Florentine Spinach Tart, p. 26
with Italian Antipasto, p. 23

Rome, Italy

Melon with Prosciutto

I have lived through two summers in Rome, under the sweltering, scorching sun. Summer is Rome's season of juicy, ripe, and fragrant melons. They are cooled and served draped with prosciutto to begin the Italian supper. The Romans dine late in the evening when the sultry sun has set. It is then that this classic Italian combination of velvety fruit and slightly salty smoked ham is at the peak of sublimity.

1 RIPE CANTALOUPE OR HONEYDEW MELON, LIGHTLY CHILLED (OR 2 FIGS OR PEARS, LIGHTLY CHILLED)

8 SLICES THINLY SLICED PROSCIUTTO (DRY-CURED SPICED ITALIAN HAM)

FRESHLY GROUND PEPPER (OPTIONAL)

If using pears, rub them lightly with lemon juice to prevent discoloring.

Peel the melon, and remove seeds. Cut into 8 thin crescent slices. If using figs, peel and cut into quarters. If using pears, quarter but don't peel.

Prosciutto is usually purchased thinly sliced from a delicatessen, or sometimes it is prepackaged in slices. In either case, the size is too large for this appetizer. You will need to use a pair of scissors to cut the prosciutto to desired shape, and then drape it over the fruit. This may be covered with plastic wrap and chilled until serving time.

In Rome, it is usually served at a cool room temperature for top flavor. A few twists of ground pepper is popular as a garnish. If you have fresh grape or fig leaves, they make an attractive lining for the serving dish.

Serves 4 to 8, depending on which fruit you use.

COLD/COOL

Tangy, Zappy Marinated Vegetables

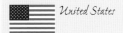 *United States*

One of the easiest and most versatile appetizers is fresh vegetables marinated in a tangy sauce. An added bonus is that when the vegetables are gone, the marinade may be used as a salad dressing! Almost any variety of vegetable may be used— even black or green canned olives. This is the basic recipe, which may be increased for larger parties.

SALT FOR BOILING WATER

½ CUP OLIVE OIL

½ CUP RED OR WHITE WINE VINEGAR, OR ¼ CUP VINEGAR AND ¼ CUP FRESH
    LEMON JUICE (SQUEEZED FROM 2 MEDIUM LEMONS)

2 CLOVES GARLIC, PEELED AND CRUSHED

1 TEASPOON DRIED OREGANO

1 TEASPOON SALT

½ TEASPOON CRUSHED, DRIED RED PEPPER

1 POUND FRESH (OR CANNED) VEGETABLES, SUCH AS MUSHROOMS, ZUCCHINI
    (CUT LENGTHWISE IN 3-INCH BY ¾-INCH STRIPS), CARROT STRIPS,
    EGGPLANT STRIPS, STRING BEANS, AND CANNED OLIVES (6 OUNCES)

Fill a saucepan or pot (large enough to hold all the vegetables) more than halfway with water, and sprinkle several dashes of salt into the water. Set on stove to boil. Meanwhile, mix together the rest of the ingredients except the vegetables in a large bowl. Set aside. When salted water is boiling, place the fresh vegetables (not the canned ones) in the water; simmer and stir for 5 minutes. Drain fresh vegetables and, while still warm, mix into the "zappy" marinade. If using olives or other canned vegetables, drain and mix into the marinade. Chill covered in the refrigerator. This will keep for up to a week.

To serve, remove vegetables from the marinade. It helps to bring the dish to room temperature for easier removal because olive oil congeals when it is cold.

This will serve 6.

Olives are especially tasty in this recipe. Father Junipero Serra and his Franciscans brought olives to California from Mexico in 1769. They were planted in all the mission gardens. This popular black variety is still called the mission olive.

COLD/COOL

 *Sicily, Italy*

Nan's Caponata

While caponata is a traditional recipe from Sicily, my friend Nan has her own savory version.

⅔ CUP OLIVE OIL

1 CLOVE GARLIC, MINCED

1 LARGE EGGPLANT

2 TEASPOONS SALT

1 CUP ONION, CHOPPED

½ CUP GREEN PEPPER, DICED

½ CUP CELERY, DICED

½ CUP SLICED BLACK OR GREEN OLIVES, DRAINED

1 TABLESPOON CAPERS

1 (14- OR 15-OUNCE) CAN PLUM TOMATOES, NOT DRAINED

2 TEASPOONS DRIED OREGANO

1 TEASPOON FRESH OR DRIED BASIL

5 TABLESPOONS WINE VINEGAR

¼ CUP TOASTED, SHELLED PINE NUTS

Pine nuts, because of their natural oil, can turn rancid easily. To keep them at peak freshness, simply store in the freezer. They will last for up to 6 months.

Heat oil with garlic in a large, heavy frying pan. Meanwhile, dice the eggplant in 1½-inch by ½-inch pieces, leaving skin on. Sauté until golden brown. Sprinkle with salt and remove from pan. In the same pan, sauté the onions, green pepper, and celery just until limp (add more oil if necessary). Stir in the olives, capers, tomatoes, seasonings, wine vinegar, and pine nuts.

Return the eggplant to the skillet. Simmer, uncovered, for 20 minutes, stirring now and then. Remove from the pan and place in a pretty bowl. Refrigerate.

Serve slightly chilled, with bread or crackers. This will keep a week in the refrigerator.

It will serve 6.

COLD/COOL

Italy

Italian Antipasto

Nearly everyone has had the pleasure, at one time or another, of encountering an *antipasto*—a large platter brought to the table, heaped with delectable morsels. This Italian word simply means "before the pasta," which is a way of saying "a little something to nibble on before the main plates of food arrive."

There is no exact recipe for this appetizer, as the components and arrangement of the dish are left to the imagination and whim of the cook. An *antipasti assorti* tray may have tuna, anchovies, sardines, little shrimp, hard-boiled eggs cut in quarters, marinated vegetables, bean salad, marinated mushrooms, salami, prosciutto, sliced tomatoes, marinated eggplant, artichoke hearts, green or red pepper strips, and other imaginative foods. Like any artistic creation, an antipasto should be original and beautiful. Composing seductive arrangements of tempting food to share with others is an art form anyone might enjoy trying.

A trip to your local delicatessen can provide all you need to create an antipasto at home. Select a variety of cheeses, meats, and marinated vegetables. Arrange them in a stylish manner on a platter. The platter may be lined with lettuce, grape leaves, or parsley, to serve as a green backdrop for the foods. Serve with fresh sliced bread or breadsticks.

To create a festive Italian mood, place the antipasto platter on a red-and-white checkered tablecloth. Serve with a choice of a chilled white Italian wine, such as Pinot Grigio, or a red Barbera (room temperature). A fresh bouquet of flowers will complete the spirit.

COLD/COOL

 *United States*

Spinach-filled Mushrooms

Mushroom appetizers always have a certain elegance. The flavors are subtle, and the round shape is perfect for fillings. Mushroom appetizers may easily be prepared ahead and served warm or cool.

12 MEDIUM TO LARGE FRESH MUSHROOMS

1 (10-OUNCE) PACKAGE FROZEN CHOPPED SPINACH

1 (3-OUNCE) PACKAGE CREAM CHEESE

1 WHOLE GREEN ONION, FINELY CHOPPED

¼ TEASPOON SALT

¼ TEASPOON PEPPER

PINCH NUTMEG

BUTTER AND OLIVE OIL FOR FRYING (USE ⅛ CUP OF EACH MIXED TOGETHER, ADDING MORE IF NEEDED)

Be sure when selecting mushrooms that the cap is closed tight to the stem. You should not be able to see the "gills." As mushrooms mature, the caps open, and they lose moisture and flavor.

Remove stems from mushrooms. Wash gently. Lightly pat dry with a paper towel.

Cook the spinach as per package directions. Press through a strainer to remove all excess juice. This step is necessary to keep the filling mixture from being runny. In a medium-sized bowl, mash spinach with cream cheese, onion, and seasonings using a fork. Fill each mushroom cavity with the spinach mixture.

Heat butter and oil in a frying pan. Lightly fry the mushrooms on the bottom side only, just until hot and light brown. These may be served hot, at room temperature, or even cold. Refrigerated, they will keep 4 days.

Usually people want several mushrooms, so plan on serving 3 to 4.

HOT/WARM

Sicilian Artichoke Tart

Sicily, Italy

Artichokes are curious and beautiful plants. The bud is the edible part. If left on the bush, it will leisurely open and turn into a dramatic, purple, thistlelike flower. This blossom is a great favorite of flower arrangers, who grow artichokes only for their blooms.

In the Mediterranean climate of Sicily, artichokes as a crop flourish. They are used in many inventive ways in the island's distinctive cuisine. When I visited this ancient island, I dined at a small trattoria near the classical theater in Taormina. For an appetizer, a wedge of this tart was served with a cool glass of the famed, local white Corvo wine. Because the grapes grow from the volcanic earth, these wines are exceptional. An artichoke tart may be used as an appetizer or for a light supper or lunch dish.

This may also be prepared in an 8-inch by 8-inch pan and cut into squares.

1 (9-OUNCE) PACKAGE FROZEN ARTICHOKE HEARTS OR 1 (13- TO 14-OUNCE) CAN ARTICHOKE HEARTS

   OLIVE OIL FOR PAN

1 TABLESPOON MINCED ONION

1 TABLESPOON LEMON JUICE

1 CLOVE GARLIC, MINCED

½ CUP PARMESAN CHEESE, GRATED

   SALT AND PEPPER TO TASTE

3 EGGS, SLIGHTLY BEATEN

¼ CUP BREAD CRUMBS FOR TOPPING

   OLIVE OIL FOR TOPPING

If using frozen hearts, cook as per package directions and drain. When using canned, also drain. Cut the artichokes (frozen or canned) into small, bite-sized pieces. Prepare a 9- or 10-inch pie pan by lightly oiling sides and bottom. In medium-sized

HOT/WARM

bowl, mix together all ingredients except bread crumbs and olive oil (for topping). Place in the pie pan. Top with crumbs, and drizzle a little olive oil over top. Bake at 350° for 20 minutes. Remove and cut into wedges. Serve slightly warm, or refrigerate and serve cool. It is best served within 2 days.

This will serve 6.

Florentine Spinach Tart

One spring, while on a family camping trip in Italy, we decided to take a picnic into the Tuscany hills. In Italy a *tavola caldo* ("hot table") is somewhat like an American delicatessen, except the food is Italian-inspired. Of course these are ideal places to select ready-made edibles for picnics. These places sell wonderful and fascinating things that have been created with vegetables, and one that attracted my eye was a spinach tart. It was the star of the picnic—we all wanted more!

I did some cooking experiments when we returned home to California and came up with this version, which has proven popular.

This may also be baked in two 9-inch pans but, of course, will not be as high.

For a picnic party, add a bottle of chilled Italian Soave or Orvieto wine.

HOT/WARM

2   (10-OUNCE) PACKAGES FROZEN CHOPPED SPINACH OR 3 BUNCHES FRESH SPINACH

2   EGGS, SLIGHTLY BEATEN

¼   CUP PARMESAN CHEESE, GRATED

1   TEASPOON NUTMEG

1   CLOVE FRESH GARLIC, PEELED AND MINCED

1   TEASPOON SALT

½   TEASPOON PEPPER

1   CUP RICOTTA OR SMALL-CURD COTTAGE CHEESE

1   TABLESPOON OLIVE OIL FOR PAN

¼   CUP SHELLED PINE NUTS

This tart may be kept warm by wrapping it in a large bath towel. It is handy to keep a pretty, colorful towel just for carrying hot appetizers to festive gatherings.

If using frozen spinach, cook the spinach according to package directions. If using fresh, wash and remove the stems. Cook covered in a saucepan with only as much water as will cling to the leaves, until tender (about 5 minutes).

Cool spinach, drain well, and then squeeze dry to remove excess juice. In a medium-sized bowl, chop spinach (if not already chopped) and combine with eggs, Parmesan, nutmeg, garlic, salt, pepper, and ricotta or cottage cheese. Rub a 9- or 10-inch pie pan with olive oil. Spread mixture evenly around the pan. Top with pine nuts. Bake at 350° for 20 minutes. Cut into wedges to serve. Spinach tart is best served warm or at room temperature.

Serves approximately 6.

Exquisite Eggs,
Cheese,
Quiche,
&
Bread

Chinese Tea Eggs, p. 33
with Deviled Eggs, p. 34

Assorted & Diverse Egg Presentations

Eggs filled with flavorful ingredients are always tasteful (in every way!) and popular as appetizers. Egg appetizers offer several functional advantages; they are inexpensive, they are well-liked, and they may be prepared ahead of time.

For these eight recipes, the eggs must be hard-boiled. Although boiling an egg is proverbially the simplest kitchen operation, it actually is possible to do it wrong, with unfortunate results. However, home economists have developed a new, easy method that results in a perfect, tender egg every time.

How to Hard Boil Eggs

Place the eggs (still in shells) in a saucepan. Add sufficient cold water to cover eggs (about 1 inch above eggs). Bring to a full boil. Turn off heat. Cover and let sit covered for 20 minutes. Empty the water into your sink, and immediately run cold water over the eggs to cool them.

Not cooling the eggs or cooking them too long will result in a tough egg.

To Cut Eggs in Half

Shell eggs and use a sharp knife that has been dipped in cold water. Usually eggs are cut lengthwise for these recipes; however, they also may be cut in half horizontally to make an egg "cup."

Remember when using this excellent method for hard boiling eggs to be sure the eggs are covered tightly for the 20-minute period.

Eggs are very nutritious. They contain 13 vitamins, protein, and numerous minerals.

Springtime Spinach Eggs

 *United States*

The first time I tasted these eggs was at a friend's springtime picnic party. The flavor combination is delectable, and the look of the soft green filling in the white egg half is lovely, somehow both pristine and perky. Serve these on a platter garnished with flowers.

1   (10-OUNCE) PACKAGE CHOPPED FROZEN SPINACH, OR 1 BUNCH FRESH
      SPINACH, COOKED AND THEN FINELY CHOPPED AND DRAINED

12 EGGS, HARD-BOILED

¼   CUP MAYONNAISE

2   TABLESPOONS OLIVE OIL

2   TABLESPOONS PARMESAN CHEESE, GRATED

     SALT AND PEPPER TO TASTE

If using frozen spinach, cook the spinach as per package directions. If using fresh, rinse and cook in saucepan on stove for 4 minutes with just enough water to cling to leaves. Drain and squeeze dry. This step is most important, as excess spinach juice will make the filling runny.

Carefully shell the eggs. Slice in half lengthwise. Remove the yolks from the whites—taking care to keep the whites intact—and put the yolks in a medium bowl. Set aside the whites. Mash the yolks with the spinach, mayonnaise, oil, cheese, salt, and pepper. Fill each egg-white half with the yolk mixture. Try to do this neatly so that the white of the egg does not have the filling dribbling over it. Chill, covered with foil or plastic wrap, until serving time. This may be prepared up to 2 days ahead.

Makes 24 appetizers.

The color of the shell does not affect the flavor of the egg.

COLD/COOL

 *United States*

Pickled Bar Eggs

Perhaps you have seen these seductive-looking eggs nestled in a glass jar at a bar or delicatessen. They taste delicious with bar-type or deli-type food. If you wish to make the eggs pink, simply add 1 cup of beet juice to the pickling liquid.

2   CUPS CIDER VINEGAR OR WHITE WINE VINEGAR

½   TEASPOON CRUSHED, DRIED RED PEPPERS

1   TEASPOON BLACK PEPPERCORNS

2   TABLESPOONS SUGAR

½   TEASPOON SALT

6   EGGS, HARD-BOILED AND SHELLED

1   CUP BEET JUICE FOR PINK EGGS (OPTIONAL)

In a medium saucepan, simmer vinegar, peppers, peppercorns, sugar, salt, and beet juice together for 5 minutes. Cool slightly. Place eggs in this mixture. Store in the refrigerator in a glass jar or stainless steel bowl for 24 hours before serving. This will keep for several weeks. To serve, remove from liquid and serve whole.

Makes 6 appetizers.

There was a time in the United States when pickled eggs, pretzels, and hot dogs were offered free to bar customers. This service, called a free lunch, helped promote liquor sales.

COLD/COOL

Chinese Tea Eggs with Scallion Brushes

China

The lovely marbled appearance of these tea eggs with green scallion brushes makes a stunning appetizer.

8   EGGS, HARD-BOILED

3   TABLESPOONS BLACK TEA OR ORANGE PEKOE TEA, OR 3 TEA BAGS OF BLACK
      OR ORANGE PEKOE TEA

¼   CUP SOY SAUCE

2   TEASPOONS ANISE SEED (OPTIONAL)

1   TABLESPOON SALT

After hard boiling eggs, tap the entire egg surface with the back of a large, heavy spoon to make fine cracks so the tea mixture will be able to penetrate and create a sort of cobweb design. Place the eggs in a saucepan, and cover with water (to about 1 inch above eggs). Add remaining ingredients. Cover and cook over a very low flame for 45 minutes. Chill in this liquid overnight.

To serve, drain and peel eggs. Cut eggs in quarters (the eggs may also be offered whole, to show off the lovely variegated effect). Garnish with scallion brushes (recipe below) or sprigs of cilantro.

Makes 8 to 32 appetizers, depending on whether you serve the eggs quartered or whole.

See photo p. 28.

To Make Scallion Brushes

Trim the roots off the green onions, and cut off the tops, leaving about 3 inches of green stalk. Holding each onion firmly in one hand, make 4 cross cuts, about 1 inch deep, in the green end of each. Chill in ice water for 30 minutes or longer. The green will spread out and make "brushes." This is an attractive garnish for any appetizer.

COLD/COOL

United States

Egg shells are porous, so eggs should not be stored near strong food, such as melons and onions. Instead they should be kept stored in their original carton for freshness.

Deviled Eggs

This is *the* classic egg appetizer. They're called deviled because of the mustard, which adds a hot, spicy (devilish) flavor.

12 EGGS, HARD-BOILED

¾ CUP MAYONNAISE (OR A LITTLE MORE; THE EGGS NEED TO BE RATHER MOIST)

2 TEASPOONS DIJON MUSTARD

SALT AND PEPPER TO TASTE

3 DASHES TABASCO OR OTHER HOT SAUCE (OPTIONAL)

PIMENTO STRIPS (A TYPE OF RED PEPPER; SOLD IN VARIOUS SIZES OF GLASS JARS) OR MINCED PARSLEY FOR GARNISH

Shell eggs and cut in half lengthwise. Remove yolks, keeping egg whites intact, and in medium bowl mash yolks with remaining ingredients except pimento strips and parsley, using a fork. Spoon into egg whites. Garnish as desired. Refrigerate until needed.

Makes 24 appetizers.

COLD/COOL

Black-Olive Stuffed Eggs

Eggs flavored with olives are tasty, and with their vibrant black-and-yellow color combination, they look rather exciting as well. The touch of horseradish adds a little zest and surprise.

12	EGGS, HARD-BOILED AND PEELED
⅓	CUP MAYONNAISE
½	CUP CANNED CHOPPED BLACK OLIVES, WELL-DRAINED
1	TABLESPOON PREPARED HORSERADISH
	SALT AND PEPPER TO TASTE

Cut eggs in half horizontally. Remove yolks, set intact whites aside, and mash yolks with remaining ingredients. Spoon mixture back into egg whites. Keep refrigerated until needed.

Makes 24 appetizers.

Salmon-Caper Stuffed Eggs

Salmon with egg yolks is another classic combination and makes a cosmopolitan and elegant appetizer.

6	EGGS, HARD-BOILED AND CUT IN HALF LENGTHWISE
¼	CUP SMOKED SALMON, MINCED
¼	CUP CAPERS
	SALT AND PEPPER TO TASTE
¼	TO ⅓ CUP MAYONNAISE
	MINCED PARSLEY FOR GARNISH

Keeping egg whites intact, remove yolks from eggs, and mix yolks with the remaining ingredients except parsley. Fill whites with mixture, and refrigerate. Garnish with parsley before serving.

Makes 12 appetizers.

If you are not sure an egg is hard-boiled, hold it up to the light. If it is not hard-boiled, the light will shine through it.

COLD/COOL

Portugal

In Portugal, sardines are a national dish. One time while visiting this country, I was a guest at a Portuguese farm lunch. The memorable menu was simply grilled sardines served with freshly baked country bread and local rosé wine.

The season for fresh sardines is June to October.

Portuguese Sardine Stuffed Eggs

Sardines are a traditional flavoring in Portuguese food. This recipe combines them with eggs for a savory appetizer.

8   EGGS, HARD-BOILED AND PEELED

1   (3¾-OUNCE) CAN SARDINES IN OIL, RINSED AND DRAINED

4   TABLESPOONS MAYONNAISE

1   TABLESPOON FRESH PARSLEY, MINCED

1   TABLESPOON LEMON JUICE

1   TABLESPOON DIJON MUSTARD

    FRESH SPINACH LEAVES AND QUARTERED CHERRY TOMATOES
      FOR GARNISH

Slice eggs in half lengthwise. Remove yolks, keeping egg whites intact, and place in a medium bowl. Set whites aside. Add remaining ingredients except spinach leaves and tomatoes to yolks. Mash and blend with a fork. Spoon mixture into egg-white halves. Refrigerate until needed. These may be made up to 2 days ahead.

To serve, place on a platter lined with spinach leaves and garnished with cherry tomatoes.

Makes 16 appetizers.

COLD/COOL

Scotch Eggs

 *Great Britain*

The first time I tasted a Scotch egg was in London, across from the British Museum in a pub, which was of course called The Museum Tavern. I saw on the counter a platter of these interesting-looking eggs, and I had to sample one. It was served cut in half on a leaf of impeccably fresh British lettuce. For me it was love at first sight.

6   EGGS, HARD-BOILED AND SHELLED

   FLOUR

1   POUND BEST-QUALITY SAUSAGE MEAT, UNCOOKED

1   UNCOOKED EGG, BEATEN, FOR COATING

   FINE BREAD CRUMBS OR CRACKER MEAL

   COOKING OIL FOR FRYING

   LETTUCE OR WATERCRESS FOR GARNISH

Pat dry eggs with a paper towel. This makes it easy for the sausage to adhere to the egg. Dip eggs in flour. Cover with a thin layer of the sausage. Brush eggs with the beaten egg. Roll gently in the crumbs or meal. There should be an even coating. You may refrigerate the eggs at this point if you wish to cook them later.

To cook, heat the oil in a frying pan. If using a nonstick pan, you will need only enough oil to coat the bottom, about ¼ inch. Fry eggs over a medium flame, on all sides, until the sausage is cooked and a golden brown. Remove from pan. Drain on a paper towel. Cut in half lengthwise, and serve on a platter with lettuce or watercress. These may be served warm or cold.

Makes 12 appetizers.

Dip your hands in water to help with patting the sausage around the egg.

COLD/COOL

France

Baked Brie or Camembert

Lightly baked Brie or Camembert is always well-liked and easy to prepare. The wheels of these cheeses will vary in size, so just use more or less almonds for a nice-looking topping. A few clusters of fresh grapes make an attractive garnish.

1   SMALL 8-INCH OR CLOSE (4½-OUNCE) WHEEL BRIE (OR CAMEMBERT)
    CHEESE

1   CUP (MORE OR LESS) SLIVERED ALMONDS, TOASTED (SEE MARGIN FOR
    TOASTING INSTRUCTIONS)

    FRENCH BREAD, SLICED

Unwrap wheel of cheese and place on a shallow, oven-proof baking dish that may be used for serving. Sprinkle almonds evenly over top surface of cheese. Place in a preheated 350° oven for about 6 to 8 minutes. The cheese should be only slightly warm and melted. Serve with French bread slices.

This will make 5 to 6 servings.

To toast nuts, place them on a baking sheet in a preheated 400° oven for 10 to 12 minutes.

HOT/WARM

Piedmont Fondue
(Fonduta)

Italy

One of our area restaurants offered a series of regional Italian dinners. On the evening the restaurant featured the Piedmont area of Italy, this savory fondue was the appetizer. It differs from the traditional Swiss fondue creations in that it is served on individual warmed plates with crostini bread instead of from a fondue pot. This *fonduta* can only be made with the distinctive Fontina cheese produced in Italy's Valle D'Aosta. The name derives from the area's Mount Fontin. This unique cheese is formed in a wheel shape and aged in well-aired stone buildings at an altitude of 10,000 feet. The white truffle used in this recipe also comes from this region and may be omitted due to its high cost.

See photo, p. 40.

ABOUT ½ POUND FONTINA CHEESE

MILK TO COVER CHEESE (ABOUT ¾ CUP)

2 TABLESPOONS BUTTER

2 EGG YOLKS

4 THIN SLICES WHITE TRUFFLE (OPTIONAL)

FRESHLY GROUND WHITE OR BLACK PEPPER, TO TASTE

CROSTINI (SEE RECIPE ON PAGE 42)

Remove the rind from the cheese (discard rind), and dice the cheese in small pieces (½ inch by ½ inch approximately). This should make 1 cup. Place cheese in a small bowl, cover with the milk, and refrigerate at least 4 hours or overnight.

To prepare, melt the butter in a double boiler over a very low flame. Drain the milk from the Fontina, reserving 2 tablespoons. Add the 2 tablespoons of milk and the cheese to the butter (discard the excess milk). Stir with a wooden spoon very slowly until melted. Add the egg yolks, one by one, to avoid curdling. Keep stirring until the mixture is smooth and shiny. If using

HOT/WARM

White truffle is a type of fleshy root that grows underground. It requires specially trained dogs or pigs to sniff out this delicacy. The Piedmont area is renowned for white truffle, which is peeled and thinly sliced into foods like fondue. It is available at fine food stores canned (year-round) and fresh (in fall). While expensive, the flavor is exquisite.

truffle, blend in 4 thin slices. Sprinkle in the pepper. Serve individually in a little mound on warmed plates, or carefully top each crostini with a little of the fondue and place on a warmed platter for serving.

This will serve 4.

Quiche Lorraine Slices or Tartlets

France

Two decades ago there was a sort of quiche plague. It was served for every occasion. Food magazines were filled with variations on the basic quiche recipe, and before long quiche became a symbol of everything fussy and snobbish. This was really too bad, as quiche (which originated in the Lorraine province of France) is a culinary classic. For a cool evening it is an ideal appetizer; it's also good as a light supper or lunch dish. Of course, there are good and bad quiches: the ones sold frozen, while convenient, cannot compare with a true freshly made quiche. Now that the fad has faded into memory, it's time to restore this classic to our appetizer menus!

UNBAKED 9-INCH PIE CRUST TO FIT A PAN AT LEAST 1½ INCHES DEEP
(USE YOUR FAVORITE PIE CRUST RECIPE OR SEE RECIPE ON PAGE 42)

6 SLICES UNCOOKED BACON, OR ¾ TO 1 CUP CUBED CANADIAN BACON
(½-INCH CUBES)

1 CUP SWISS CHEESE, GRATED

3 EGGS

¼ TEASPOON NUTMEG

SALT AND PEPPER TO TASTE

PINCH CAYENNE

2 CUPS CREAM AND/OR HALF AND HALF

Ceramic quiche pans are available in many stores and are a handy piece of kitchen equipment to have.

Fill pie pan or four 2-inch tartlet pans with pie crust. Heat oven to 375°. If using bacon, fry just until barely crisp. Drain on paper towels and crumble. Place bacon or Canadian bacon cubes on bottom of pie crust(s). Sprinkle with the cheese. In a medium bowl, mix remaining ingredients with a whisk until well blended and carefully pour into crust(s). Bake 45 to 50 minutes. Bake tartlets 30 minutes. The quiche should be golden brown and slightly firm. Do

HOT/WARM

Italy

not worry if the quiche is not completely firm when removed from oven; it firms as it cools. Let stand for at least 10 minutes on a wire rack before serving.

Cut into 8 serving pieces.

Quiche Crust

1½ CUPS FLOUR

¼ CUP VEGETABLE SHORTENING

¼ CUP BUTTER, COOL

¼ TEASPOON SALT

¼ CUP (+ 1 TABLESPOON IF NEEDED) COLD MILK OR WATER

FLOUR FOR SURFACE

Place flour in a medium bowl, and add shortening, butter, and salt. Blend with a pastry blender, fork, or hands until the mixture is like a coarse meal. Add liquid, and with your hands form a ball. Place the dough on a cool, floured surface (marble is best). With a rolling pin, flatten dough into a circle large enough to fit the baking pan to its edges. Place in the pie or quiche pan or cut to fit tartlet pans.

Crostini

See recipe for Piedmont Fondue, pp. 39–40, for a tasty accompaniment to crostini bread.

HOT/WARM

Crostini is a toasted bread that may be used with spreads or served plain as an accompaniment to appetizers. The bread is toasted or broiled on one or both sides, until lightly browned as desired, before the topping is added.

LONG LOAF FRENCH BAGUETTE OR ITALIAN BREAD (MAY BE PARTIALLY FROZEN FOR EASIER SLICING)

Slice the bread into ¼-inch-thick slices. Put bread slices on baking sheet, and place in 400° oven for 4 to 6 minutes until lightly browned. This may also be toasted by broiling bread about 4 inches from heat. Remove from oven, turn bread slices over, and repeat on other side (if you want both sides toasted). The crostini may be served warm, or it may be cooled and stored in an airtight container until needed. If you plan to add a topping, do so right before serving.

One of the best and most popular toppings for crostini is a simple mixture of chopped fresh tomato combined with minced fresh basil leaves and garlic. To add this topping, combine the three in a bowl, and experiment until you find a combination that suits your tastebuds. Spread mixture on bread slices.

Italy

Bruschetta

Bruschetta is simply toast, flavored with garlic and olive oil. It is uncomplicated and unpretentious. Originally, in Italy, the toasted bread was used to test the first pressing of the year's olive oil (it was dipped in the oil and then eaten).

- 2 CLOVES FRESH GARLIC, PEELED
  SALT AND PEPPER TO TASTE
- ¼ CUP OLIVE OIL
- 6 MEDIUM SLICES FIRM ITALIAN-STYLE WHITE BREAD

Bruschetta has traditionally been used as sustenance for impoverished Italian citizens.

Place the garlic between two sheets of waxed paper or plastic wrap. Mash with a pounding tool until the garlic is finely squashed. Scrape the garlic off the paper, and in a small bowl combine with salt, pepper, and oil. Brush over top side of the bread. Broil on a baking sheet 3 to 4 inches from heat for about 2 minutes until toasted golden brown. This bread may also be baked in a 350° oven for about 8 minutes or grilled over a charcoal fire. Bruschetta is typically served as a nibble with a glass of pre-dinner wine.

Makes 6 slices.

HOT/WARM

Upscale Finger Food

Tiny Potatoes with Tasty Toppings, p. 55

Nuts to Nibble

Nuts are the perfect appetizer staple. It is always easy to store canned or bottled nuts on your kitchen shelves. They may be served straight out of their containers or in one of these variations. Use attractive wooden bowls for serving.

 United States

Toasted, Salted Nuts

2   CUPS RAW WALNUTS, ALMONDS, OR PECANS (NO SHELLS)
1   TABLESPOON SWEET BUTTER (BUTTER WITHOUT ADDED SALT), ROOM
      TEMPERATURE
1   TEASPOON KOSHER OR IODIZED SALT

Spread nuts on a baking sheet. Bake in a preheated 300° oven about 15 to 20 minutes or until slightly brown. Stir around while baking, and watch carefully. Remove from oven, and toss with butter and salt while hot.

 Mexico

Mexican Nuts

4   CUPS WALNUT HALVES (NO SHELLS)
¼   CUP BUTTER, MELTED
1   TABLESPOON CHILI POWDER
2   TEASPOONS CUMIN
1   TEASPOON SALT

Place nuts on a baking sheet, cover with butter, and stir to coat. Bake in preheated oven, 12 minutes at 350°. Sprinkle with chili powder, cumin, and salt. Stir around, and bake an additional 5 minutes.

COLD/COOL

 *United States*

This is a fresh and interesting nibble.

Walnut-Cheese Sandwiches

½ CUP (**4** OUNCES) BLUE CHEESE, ROOM TEMPERATURE

½ CUP (**4** OUNCES) SWEET BUTTER, (BUTTER WITHOUT ADDED SALT),
     ROOM TEMPERATURE

24 WALNUT HALVES, SHELLED

Blend the cheese and butter. Chill 30 minutes. Dab the mixture between two walnut halves. Press halves together. Serve within the hour.

Makes 12 appetizers.

COLD/COOL

47

Assorted Sandwiches

Tiny, delectable sandwiches are a good choice for appetizers. These are especially useful for large parties and receptions, as they may be prepared ahead and refrigerated; it is easy to refill your serving trays as needed. To keep the sandwiches at peak freshness while refrigerated, wrap in foil or plastic wrap and place a dampened dish towel over them.

The presentation of this food is important. Platters garnished with fresh flowers and attractive leaves (lettuce, grape, or fig) will serve as a striking background. Use your imagination to create an exciting arrangement.

 *Great Britain*

Cucumber and salmon sandwiches are good choices for wedding showers or receptions. Garnish the platters with white roses. Place sandwiches on cake stands for an attractive presentation.

COLD/COOL

Cucumber Sandwiches

1   LONG ENGLISH-STYLE CUCUMBER (OR 2 MEDIUM)
    SALT TO TASTE
12 SLICES STURDY WHITE OR WHEAT SQUARE BREAD
1   (4-OUNCE) CUBE UNSALTED BUTTER, ROOM TEMPERATURE
    BLACK PEPPER, FRESHLY GROUND
1   (8-OUNCE) PACKAGE CREAM CHEESE, ROOM TEMPERATURE

Peel cucumber. Slice very thin. Place in a colander that has been set in the sink, and sprinkle with salt. Put a weight on top of the cucumbers (this can be a food can, cooking pot, etc.—anything that will keep the cucumbers pressed). This step drains excess liquid. Let them stand for 1 hour. Pat dry with paper or cloth towels. Butter one slice of bread, and place a layer of cucumbers on top of the butter. Sprinkle with freshly ground black pepper. Spread cream cheese on other bread slice. Place the two slices together, cream cheese against cucumbers. Trim crusts and cut sandwiches in quarters, triangles, or halves.

Makes 12 to 24 appetizers.

Salmon Sandwiches

These are a favorite of my artist daughter, Suzanne, who uses them for art gallery openings, parties, and special guests.

BREAD

BUTTER, AT ROOM TEMPERATURE FOR EASY SPREADING

SMOKED SALMON

PARSLEY, FRESH DILL, OR CAPERS FOR GARNISH (OPTIONAL)

The amount of the ingredients required will depend on the event. Remove crusts from the bread of your choice. Cut in 4 squares or triangles. For each sandwich, spread one side of one of the pieces of bread with butter. Cut a piece of salmon to fit the bread. Place on the butter. Top salmon with second piece of bread. Garnish with desired topping.

Kitchen scissors work well for cutting the salmon.

From front to back: Salmon Sandwiches and Cucumber Sandwiches.

COLD/COOL

 *United States*

Watercress Sandwiches

1 LARGE BUNCH WATERCRESS

1 (8-OUNCE) PACKAGE CREAM CHEESE, ROOM TEMPERATURE

1 (4-OUNCE) CUBE SWEET BUTTER (BUTTER WITH NO ADDED SALT), ROOM
TEMPERATURE

12 SLICES (APPROXIMATELY) WHITE OR WHEAT BREAD

SALT AND PEPPER TO TASTE

Rinse and dry the watercress. Remove the thick stems. Cut the leaves in small portions. Set aside. Blend cream cheese and butter. Spread one side of thin slices of bread with butter-and-cream-cheese mixture. Top the buttered sides of half the slices with a layer of watercress. Place the remaining bread buttered side down on top of the watercress halves, to form sandwiches. Trim off the crusts, cut each sandwich in 4 squares or triangles, and arrange on a platter.

Makes about 24 appetizers.

Lillika's Egg and Tuna Sandwiches

This tuna sandwich is my all-time favorite—simple, yet elegant enough for any occasion.

Lillika, a friend of my daughter Suzanne, comes from the Czech Republic. This recipe is unique and distinct from other tuna sandwiches because of the added typical Czech ingredients (garlic, onions, and eggs).

COLD/COOL

2 (6-OUNCE) CANS TUNA IN OIL

3 EGGS, HARD-BOILED

2 SMALL WHITE ONIONS, PEELED AND FINELY DICED

½ CUP MAYONNAISE AND MAYBE 2 TABLESPOONS EXTRA, AS MIXTURE SHOULD
   BE CREAMY AND MOIST

   ABOUT 2 TABLESPOONS LEMON JUICE FROM ½ MEDIUM-SIZED LEMON

2 GARLIC CLOVES, PEELED, MINCED, AND DICED

   SALT AND PEPPER TO TASTE

   GOOD-QUALITY, SQUARE, LARGE LOAF SANDWICH BREAD, WHITE OR WHEAT

1 (4-OUNCE) CUBE BUTTER, ROOM TEMPERATURE

   CHIVES, MINCED PARSLEY, AND/OR PAPRIKA FOR GARNISH

Czech Republic

Drain tuna, leaving a little oil for taste and moisture. Place in a medium-sized bowl. Cut the hard-boiled eggs in half lengthwise. Lay each half, yolk side down, in a medium-fine strainer, and press the eggs through to the bowl of tuna. Next add onions, mayonnaise, lemon juice, and garlic to the mixture. Blend together with a fork. Mash and mix until fluffy. Add salt and pepper to taste. Add more mayonnaise if needed. Mashing and mixing well with the fork will give the mixture its characteristic fluffiness. This may be done up to a day ahead and refrigerated.

To assemble sandwiches, trim crusts from good-quality sandwich bread. Spread a thin layer of butter on one side of each slice. Next spread the tuna mixture generously on each slice (these are open-faced sandwiches). Cut in fourths or triangles, depending on the event and the number of people. Garnish with a few snips of chives, minced parsley, or paprika to add zest and color. A checkerboard design of one sandwich with paprika and one with chives or parsley is attractive.

Serves 8.

Beer is the national beverage of the Czech Republic. The Pilsner variety is recognized as one of the world's finest. It has been brewed in Pilsen since the Middle Ages. A selection of Czech beers is a nice accompaniment with these sandwiches.

COLD/COOL

 *United States*

Roll-ups

Roll-ups are easy and fun to assemble. Always popular, they look undeniably tempting on the appetizer platter. The measurements in these next three recipes are approximate, as the beef, turkey, or salmon slices may vary in size.

Roast Beef with Horseradish

Roll-ups are especially useful appetizers because they may be created in advance.

1   (8-OUNCE) PACKAGE CREAM CHEESE, ROOM TEMPERATURE
3   TABLESPOONS PREPARED HORSERADISH (SOLD IN GLASS JARS; THIS IS A
     MIXTURE OF HORSERADISH ROOTS AND VINEGAR)
3   TABLESPOONS FINELY CHOPPED CHIVES OR GREEN-ONION TOPS
⅓   CUP SOUR CREAM
     SALT AND PEPPER TO TASTE
16 THIN SLICES RARE ROAST BEEF

Place the cream cheese, horseradish, chives or onions, and sour cream in a medium bowl. Blend together until smooth; add salt and pepper to taste. Spread a nice layer, ¼ inch thick, on each beef slice. Roll up. The rolls may be cut in halves or thirds. It may be necessary to fasten each roll-up with a toothpick.

Makes 32 to 48 appetizers, depending on whether you cut roll-ups into halves or thirds.

COLD/COOL

Salmon with Cream Cheese & Capers

 *United States*

1   (3-OUNCE) PACKAGE CREAM CHEESE, ROOM TEMPERATURE
2   TABLESPOONS PREPARED HORSERADISH (SOLD IN GLASS JARS; THIS IS A
      MIXTURE OF HORSERADISH ROOTS AND VINEGAR)
    BLACK PEPPER, FRESHLY GROUND TO TASTE
2   TEASPOONS CAPERS, MASHED
8   THIN SLICES SMOKED SALMON

Blend all ingredients except salmon. Lay salmon slices out, and gently spread each slice with a layer of mixture. Carefully roll up, using a toothpick to secure roll if necessary.

This will make 8 rolls.

Turkey with Blue Cheese

8   OUNCES BLUE CHEESE, ROOM TEMPERATURE
1   (8-OUNCE) PACKAGE CREAM CHEESE, ROOM TEMPERATURE
⅓   CUP SOUR CREAM
1   CLOVE GARLIC, PEELED AND MINCED
    SALT AND PEPPER TO TASTE
8   THIN SLICES TURKEY BREAST
    WATERCRESS OR PARSLEY SPRIGS FOR GARNISH

Blend the cheeses, sour cream, garlic, salt, and pepper. Spread a layer of mixture on each turkey slice, and roll up. These may be cut in smaller portions if desired. Serve garnished with sprigs of watercress or parsley.

Makes approximately 8 to 32 appetizers, depending on how many portions you cut each roll-up into.

Capers are the unopened buds of the caper plant (capparis spinosa), which is a native of the Mediterranean. These tiny buds are picked when tightly closed. They are then salted and preserved in a vinegar mixture.

COLD/COOL

To grow endive, the plant is first grown to maturity. Then the leaves are discarded. The remaining root is then buried in sand and kept in a dark place. The shoots produced by these roots are called chicons. When these pointed cylinders reach a height of about 6 inches, they are harvested.

When selecting, look for firm, tightly closed, creamy-white endives.

COLD/COOL

Endive with Caviar

Endive, a member of the chicory plant family, was originally imported to this country from Belgium. Today it is grown in the United States and has become a multimillion-dollar business.

Pale, glossy endive leaves, arranged on a plate with a spoonful of glistening caviar on each leaf, make a regal sight. This elegant appetizer is a peerless accompaniment for sparkling champagne.

2 BELGIAN ENDIVES
2 TABLESPOONS BLACK CAVIAR
2 TABLESPOONS RED CAVIAR

Gently wash the endive. Select 10 to 12 of the largest leaves (the remaining leaves can be used for salad). Arrange on a plate with the tips facing outward. Divide the caviar among the leaves, with red on one and black on another. You will need just a dab on the inside of each leaf. Of course, if you want to use all one color caviar, that's fine, but it is attractive to use the alternating colors.

Makes 10 to 12 appetizers.

Tiny Potatoes with Tasty Toppings

Can anyone resist a little red or white new potato, dolloped with sour cream and caviar? I have seen these morsels disappear from appetizer trays in what seemed like seconds. Sour cream and caviar are not the only toppings that can be used; the little potatoes are just as seductive when accompanied by a tiny pink shrimp, a spoonful of chopped olives, or a dab of guacamole.

12 SMALL RED OR WHITE NEW POTATOES, UNPEELED

1 CUP SOUR CREAM

    TOPPINGS: CAVIAR, SHRIMP, GUACAMOLE, CHOPPED OLIVES, ETC.

Wash the potatoes. Boil or steam until barely tender, about 20 minutes. Do not overcook. Drain and cool slightly. Cut a thin slice from the bottom of each potato. This will help it sit evenly on your serving platter. Cut off the top of each potato. Scoop out a small hollow (about the size of a tablespoon) from the center. For convenience, this step may be done ahead; simply cover potatoes with foil, and refrigerate until ready to fill.

To serve, place a spoonful of sour cream in each cavity, with desired topping. The potatoes may be served slightly warm or chilled—this recipe is versatile! You can also set out bowls of the toppings and let guests fill their own potatoes.

Makes 12 appetizers.

This appetizer is a good choice for large parties. Accompany it with champagne, which adds a festive mood to any celebration. Place the bottles in a large container filled with ice.

See photo, p. 44.

HOT/WARM

Mexico

Terrific Nachos

Nachos are so addictive that everyone loves them. Nibbled everywhere in public places and at sporting events, nachos are also a winner for parties at home. This easy, last-minute appetizer is fun and deceptively simple to prepare. The keys to success are sturdy chips and good-quality cheese.

30 OR MORE WEDGE-SHAPED CORN TORTILLA CHIPS

1½ CUPS MONTEREY JACK OR SHARP CHEDDAR CHEESE, GRATED

1 (4-OUNCE) CAN THINLY SLICED JALAPEÑO PEPPERS, DRAINED, OR 4 TO 5 FRESH JALEPEÑOS, THINLY SLICED (CANNED ARE USUALLY USED, ALTHOUGH FRESH MAY BE SUBSTITUTED; THE NAME ON THE CAN WILL BE JALAPEÑOS EN ESCABECHE)

LIME WEDGES (OPTIONAL)

You can also dab the chips with a small amount of refried beans before the cheese is added.

Place the tortilla chips close together on a cookie sheet or in an oven-proof dish. Sprinkle the cheese evenly over the chips. Place under the broiler until the cheese is bubbling and light brown. Scatter the jalapeños over the nachos according to your taste. Serve immediately in the same dish, garnished with lime wedges if desired. Lime juice adds extra zap and zest and is squeezed individually over nachos.

This will serve 6 to 7.

HOT/WARM

Josefinas

 *United States*

You may have tasted Josefinas at a party. Guests rapidly devour these morsels and compliment the cook. It comes as a pleasant surprise to find that this appetizer is easy to assemble. Josefinas can be handy for entertaining unexpected guests because the ingredients are always in your kitchen.

¼ CUP PARMESAN CHEESE, GRATED

¼ CUP MAYONNAISE

2 TABLESPOONS FINELY MINCED GREEN ONIONS OR 1 SMALL ONION

7 SLICES FIRM-TEXTURED WHITE BREAD

Combine cheese and enough mayonnaise to make a firm spread with green onions. If using white onions, cut paper thin rounds no larger than 2 inches in diameter. Cut 2-inch bread circles with a cookie cutter or scissors. You should be able to get two rounds from each bread slice. Toast bread circles on one side by placing under broiler until light brown. Spread mixture on toasted side of each round. If using white onions, place one onion circle on each round. These are open-faced sandwiches. Place under broiler and broil just until delicately brown and puffy, 2 to 3 minutes. Watch that they do not burn.

This will make 14 rounds. While this recipe serves only approximately 4 people, it is a convenient amount. For a party, the recipe may be enlarged.

The mayo mixture and bread rounds may be prepared ahead, but do not spread mixture on bread until time to cook.

HOT/WARM

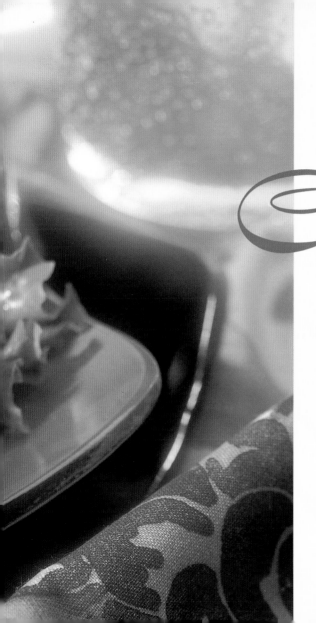

*First-Class
Fish, Meat,
&
Poultry
Appetizers*

Hanalei Bay Shrimp, p. 62

New Orleans' French Market is America's oldest continuously operated city marketplace. It has dazzling displays of local foods, street musicians, and artisans. The aroma of dark New Orleans coffee fills the air. Sit down and enjoy the mood while sipping a cup of this tempting brew at the market's famed Café du Monde.

COLD/COOL

Brennan's Shrimp Remoulade

In the South, a cool and pretty dish of shrimp remoulade is often served as an appetizer. The best remoulade I ever found was in New Orleans at Brennan's famous restaurant on Royal Street. To dine on the charming patio amid tropical plants while nibbling fresh gulf shrimp, mingled with the restaurant's perfect sauce, is an enchanting moment. The gracious Brennan family members, renowned for their Southern hospitality, offered to share their own recipe for this classic dish.

½ CUP CELERY, MINCED

⅓ CUP SCALLION TOPS, MINCED

⅓ CUP PARSLEY, MINCED

¼ CUP DILL PICKLES, MINCED

2 TABLESPOONS GARLIC, MINCED

½ CUP CREOLE MUSTARD

2 TEASPOONS HORSERADISH (OR TO TASTE)

½ CUP VEGETABLE OIL

¼ CUP RED WINE VINEGAR

1 TABLESPOON WORCESTERSHIRE SAUCE

PINCH SALT

PINCH WHITE PEPPER

8 LARGE ROMAINE LETTUCE LEAVES

2 CUPS ICEBERG LETTUCE, SHREDDED

48 (1 POUND) MEDIUM SHRIMP, BOILED AND CHILLED (SEE BOILING INSTRUCTIONS ON PAGE 61)

Combine all the ingredients, through the white pepper, in a large mixing bowl. Stir until well blended, and then chill this remoulade sauce in the refrigerator for 2 hours.

To serve, place a lettuce leaf on each of 8 plates, and top with about ¼ cup shredded lettuce. Arrange 6 boiled shrimp on

each plate on top of the lettuce. Drizzle with 2 tablespoons remoulade sauce.

Makes 8 appetizers.

Boiling Shrimp

Brennan's boils its shrimp in a stock pot with a gallon of water, 3 large lemons (halved), 2 large bay leaves, 1½ teaspoons cayenne pepper, 1½ teaspoons black pepper, 5 tablespoons salt, 2 garlic cloves (peeled), and one 3-ounce bag of crab boil (optional). This will be ample for 3 pounds of shrimp. Boiled shrimp take approximately 6 minutes to cook. (Bring stock in pot to a boil before adding shrimp.)

Kauai, Hawaii

*Kauai is the farthest
Hawaiian island in the
Pacific. Because of this
distant position, the nightly
stars make you feel as if
you can reach up and
caress the constellations.*

Hanalei Bay Shrimp

Alluring Hanalei Bay is located on the northern shore of the Hawaiian island of Kauai. One year we celebrated Valentine's Day at the nearby Princeville Hotel. After a long, hectic, frazzled day of airplane travel, we arrived just in time to watch the spectacular sunset from the Cafe Hanalei. We began our dinner with the chilled Shrimp Hanalei and a cool glass of Sauvignon Blanc wine. This combination of large shrimp garnished with fresh island fruit and resting on a lettuce bouquet was enchanting. Of course I wanted the recipe! In the gracious island spirit of *aloha,* the hotel's executive chef, Anthony Layton-Matthews, offered to share his recipe.

Ingredients for Cooking Shrimp

3	CUPS WATER
1	LEMON, CUT IN HALF
1	CUP DRY WHITE WINE
	SALT AND PEPPER TO TASTE
2	BAY LEAVES
10	BLACK PEPPERCORNS
20	LARGE SHRIMP (15 COUNT PER POUND)

In a large pot, combine all the ingredients except shrimp. Bring to a boil, and add shrimp. Boil for 5 minutes, until the shrimp are firm and bright red but not overcooked. Remove the shrimp and place in a freezer for 15 minutes to cool off. Do not use ice water to cool the shrimp, as it will dilute the flavor of the shrimp. When the shrimp are cool, peel and devein them. Set aside.

COLD/COOL

Ingredients for Salsa

1   MEDIUM PAPAYA, PEELED AND DICED
1   MEDIUM MANGO, PEELED AND DICED
¼   RED ONION, PEELED AND FINELY DICED
1   TABLESPOON FRESH CILANTRO, CHOPPED
    JUICE FROM 1 LIME
1   TABLESPOON RED PEPPER, FINELY DICED

Combine ingredients in a bowl and refrigerate.

Ingredients for Serving with Lettuce Bouquet

2   CUPS ASSORTED MIXED BABY LETTUCE, TO INCLUDE BABY RED LEAF,
    MIZUNA, MANCHE, AND FRISEE AND SPOON SPINACH
4   OUNCES THAI SWEET CHILI SAUCE (AVAILABLE IN FINE SUPERMARKETS)
1   LEMON, CUT IN WEDGES

See photo, p. 58.

Arrange greens by layering each leaf to form beautiful lettuce bouquets, similar to a flower arrangement.

To Serve

On each serving plate, place one lettuce bouquet, gently rest 4 shrimp around the lettuce, and spoon the salsa decoratively around the shrimp. To finish, simply top each shrimp with the Thai chili sauce and garnish with fresh lemon.

This will serve 5.

 *United States*

Becky's Shrimp in Spinach Leaves

This delicate combination from my dear friend Becky is a winner.

ABOUT 20 FRESH LARGE SPINACH LEAVES, WASHED (SEE MARGIN FOR WASHING INSTRUCTIONS)
1 (3-OUNCE) PACKAGE CREAM CHEESE, ROOM TEMPERATURE
¼ POUND COOKED BAY SHRIMP, COARSELY CHOPPED
1 TABLESPOON FRESH CILANTRO, MINCED
1 TABLESPOON PREPARED HORSERADISH
2 DROPS TABASCO SAUCE

Steam the spinach leaves by placing in a steamer basket with 1½ inches of water under basket. Steam for 1 to 2 minutes, just until the leaves are barely limp. Set aside. In a medium bowl, cream the cheese until fluffy. Add remaining ingredients. Divide mixture among the leaves, placing mixture in center. Fold over the sides of the leaves to make a roll enclosing the filling. Chill and serve.

Makes about 20 appetizers.

To easily wash spinach, first remove roots and any tough stems. Run cool tap water over spinach in your sink for the preliminary rinse. Then place leaves in a large bowl. Cover with cool water. Let soak a few minutes, and then swish leaves around. Any dirt will fall to the bottom of the bowl. Repeat process if needed. Remove leaves from the water and drain.

COLD/COOL

Salmon Party Loaf

 *United States*

I like recipes that make a smart and spiffy impression. It is another plus if the dish can be prepared ahead. This flavorful creation offers both of these advantages and is an attractive choice for wedding showers or buffets.

1   (15-OUNCE OR CLOSE) CAN SALMON

1   (8-OUNCE) PACKAGE CREAM CHEESE

2   TEASPOONS GRATED OR FINELY MINCED WHITE ONION

1   TABLESPOON FRESH LEMON JUICE

1   TABLESPOON PREPARED HORSERADISH

¼   TEASPOON LIQUID SMOKE

½   CUP FINELY CHOPPED WALNUTS OR PECANS

3   TABLESPOONS FINELY SNIPPED PARSLEY

Drain the canned salmon, and put in a medium-sized bowl. Pick out any bones or dark pieces of skin. Add remaining ingredients except nuts and parsley, and mix well. Chill for several hours until firm. Mold into a "log." In another bowl, combine nuts and parsley. Carefully roll the log in nut-and-parsley combination. Place on a serving dish and chill. This will keep 2 days in the refrigerator. Serve with crackers or rye toast.

Serves 5 to 6 people.

A pair of sharp kitchen scissors is a perfect tool for snipping parsley, America's most popular garnish. Fresh flowers will also make an attractive garnish for this salmon loaf. Pansies look especially pleasing.

COLD/COOL

Paris, France

Paris Terrine

When I lived in Paris, every day I shopped for food because we did not have a refrigerator and because it is a French custom. At first I was a little apprehensive about buying things because my high school French was tottery. The street I did my marketing on was Rue Lepic, which winds and curves up to the top of the Montmartre hill. Along this route is an extensive maze of alluring and tempting things to cook and eat.

One of my first memorable adventures on this famed street was my first visit to a *charcuterie* (a kind of French delicatessen). As I strolled through the door, the mingled aromas of spices, pickles, and marinating meats inundated my senses. My eyes viewed a scene of mouth-watering pâtés and terrines, topped with shimmering aspic glaze or frilled pastry toppings, all lined up in a neat row. Hanging on the walls were plump smoked hams between strings of salami and sausages. The marble counters held containers of marinated vegetables, fancifully decorated cooked eggs, prepared snails in their pretty brown and white shells, golden-brown baked quiches, and other gastronomic delicacies.

The sturdy, spirited shop ladies, adorned in a sort of white nurse's uniform, crisply inquired, *"Que desirez-vous?"* How could I respond? It was a bewilderment of endless delectable temptations. Soon I narrowed my choice down to the terrines and pâtés. Every day for lunch we would sample different kinds with a fresh baguette.

Certainly I do know there is nothing equivalent to selections fresh from a Paris charcuterie, but because I live in California this is my version of a Paris terrine. A terrine is simply an earthenware dish (*terre* is the French word for "earth") that the food is baked in. (Any combination of meat, fish, or vegetable may be prepared in a terrine. Because they are baked in this distinctive dish, the mixtures are named terrines.)

The chicken in this terrine may be a combination of thighs and breasts.

COLD/COOL

2 CUPS COOKED, DICED CHICKEN

1 POUND LEAN SAUSAGE, UNCOOKED

1½ CUPS DICED HAM

2 CLOVES GARLIC, MINCED

2 TABLESPOONS FRESH PARSLEY, MINCED

1 TEASPOON THYME

2 EGGS

¼ CUP BRANDY OR COGNAC

SALT AND PEPPER TO TASTE

½ POUND SLICED BACON

¼ CUP SHELLED PISTACHIO NUTS, CHOPPED COARSELY

BAY LEAVES OR ROSEMARY SPRIGS FOR GARNISH (OPTIONAL)

Place the chicken in a small bowl. In a larger bowl, combine sausage, ham, garlic, parsley, thyme, eggs, brandy, salt, and pepper. Line an oven casserole dish (1½- to 2-quart capacity) with the sliced bacon, reserving two slices for the top. Place the chicken in the "terrine" on top of the bacon. Cover with half of the nuts, followed by half of the sausage mixture. Sprinkle the remaining nuts over the top, and then add remaining sausage mixture. Lay the two slices of bacon across the top. You may garnish this with bay leaves or rosemary sprigs if desired.

Cover the casserole dish with foil. Make a single tiny hole in the foil for the steam to escape. Place in a larger pan of hot water. The water should come up to half the height of the casserole dish. Bake in a 375° oven for 1½ hours, adding additional water to bottom pan if needed.

Cool and refrigerate overnight. You may want to place a weight on the terrine as it cools, to make it firmer. This will keep for a week. To serve, cut desired size of slices from the terrine. The bacon may be removed from the top. Place a slice of the terrine on a plate and serve with cornichons and a basket of French bread.

This will make around 10 servings.

Cornichons are small gherkin pickles with a fine, sharp taste. They are the traditional terrine accompaniment.

Paris, France

While in Paris, enjoy a walk on the celebrated food-market streets. The favorites are Rue Lepic, Rue Mouffetard, and Rue Cler.

Rillettes de Campagne
("Country Potted Pork")

I first tasted this flavorful appetizer in a Parisian sidewalk café. The waiter brought me a small, white bowl filled with this delicious mixture along with a basket of crusty French bread. He wished me *"bon appetit"* with the cavalier spirit that is an enduring quality of Paris restaurant associates.

Basically, rillettes (pronounced ree-etts) are simply cubes of pork, mixed with seasonings and slowly baked. Certainly there

COLD/COOL

are more complicated ways of preparing rillettes; however this easy method offers a tasty result.

3 TO 4 POUNDS PORK SHOULDER (LOIN MAY BE USED, BUT INCLUDE
　　 AT LEAST ¼ CUP PORK FAT)

　 SALT AND PEPPER TO TASTE

1 TEASPOON THYME (FRESH OR DRIED)

1 BAY LEAF

2 CLOVES GARLIC, MINCED

½ CUP WATER

¾ CUP DRY WHITE WINE

Cut the pork into 1½-inch cubes. Place in a heavy pot (that will fit in your oven) with remaining ingredients. Stir to blend ingredients. Cover, and bake at 250°, stirring now and then. The idea is to have the liquid slowly cook away from the pork. When the liquid is absorbed, the rillettes will be done. This will take 3½ to 4 hours. Carefully watch, toward the end of the cooking, that the pork does not burn on the bottom.

Remove from oven, and cool slightly. With two forks, shred the pork. You want a coarse, not a mushy, texture. Taste for seasoning. Usually it tastes best a little overseasoned. Place in crockery pots or pretty small bowls, and cover with foil or plastic wrap. The fat will rise to the top and act as a preservative. Refrigerate. This will keep for a week to 10 days.

Discard fat, and serve from bowl or pot with bread or crackers (as a spread) and cornichons (little sour pickles) if desired.

This recipe will make 4 small bowls.

Personally, I like my rillettes to have a peppery taste, so you may want to add additional pepper and salt if needed.

Sonoma Valley,
California

Sonoma Valley Shrimp Toast

Northern California's Sonoma Valley is the home of many renowned vineyards. In the center of this pastoral valley is the historical town of Sonoma, which has a mission, vintage homes, and the classic city plaza. The streets are lined with restaurants and specialty food shops. Because many of this area's original settlers came from Northern Italy, local restaurants reflect this heritage. Shrimp toast is one of Sonoma's popular appetizers.

½ POUND BABY BAY SHRIMP, COOKED

½ CUP GRATED PARMESAN CHEESE

2 TABLESPOONS FRESH LEMON JUICE

½ TEASPOON DRIED OR FRESH THYME

1 TABLESPOON FRESH MINCED PARSLEY

½ CUP MAYONNAISE

1 TEASPOON CAPERS, MINCED

SALT AND PEPPER TO TASTE

6 SLICES STURDY WHITE BREAD, TOASTED LIGHTLY AND BUTTERED

FRESH MINCED PARSLEY FOR GARNISH

Baby bay shrimp are usually sold cooked. However if you should purchase raw shrimp, simply place them in a medium-sized saucepan filled with 4 cups boiling salted water. Cook for 3 minutes over a medium flame. Drain immediately.

Chop the shrimp medium-fine. For this recipe you want a little texture, not a mush. Add the remaining ingredients (except bread), and mix together. This may be prepared ahead and kept refrigerated for up to 2 days.

Remove crusts from the toasted, buttered bread if desired and cut in half. Spread shrimp mixture evenly on the buttered side of each piece of toast. Gently pat down so it looks tidy. Place on a

Keep bay shrimp in ½-pound packages in your freezer so you can create this delectable toast on the spur of the moment. A chilled bottle of Sauvignon Blanc wine is the consummate accompaniment for this appetizer.

HOT/WARM

baking sheet, and bake at 350° until hot and bubbly, about 8 minutes. Place on a platter, and garnish with a little fresh minced parsley. This appetizer is eaten using the hands rather than utensils.

This will serve 4.

United States

East-West Chicken Wings

Platters of tempting chicken wings are always well-liked. This easy recipe with subtle Asian flavoring has long been a favorite of the docents and staff of the Natural History Museum of Los Angeles. The wings are marinated, cooked, and served all from the same pot. To add a colorful elegant finish, garnish with cilantro sprigs and lime or pineapple slices.

4   POUNDS CHICKEN WINGS, WITH SKIN
1   CUP SOY SAUCE
1   CUP BROWN SUGAR
½   CUP BUTTER
1   TABLESPOON DIJON MUSTARD
¾   CUP WATER
    LIME SLICES, FRESH CILANTRO, OR DICED PINEAPPLE FOR GARNISH

Cut chicken wings at joints and discard tips. Arrange the wings in a shallow baking pan. Combine remaining ingredients, except garnishes, in a saucepan. Heat on stove at medium heat until butter and sugar mix. Stir and cool. When the sauce is cool, pour over the wings. Mix around for even coating. Refrigerate and marinate for several hours or overnight, turning wings over once or twice so marinade will penetrate them.

Bake at 350° for 50 minutes. Drain, and serve garnished, hot or cold.

This will serve 15 to 20.

Soy sauce is created from a fermentation process that blends cooked soybeans, roasted wheat, and salt. Records show this pungent sauce was made and used in China 200 years before Christ.

HOT/WARM

Carnitas with Guacamole

Mexico

Carnitas is a Spanish word that means "little pieces of meat." These crispy, seasoned morsels make a terrific appetizer. When served with guacamole, this appetizer is colorful as well as a delicious combination of flavors and textures.

1 POUND PORK SHOULDER (OR OTHER CUT OF PORK)

   SALT AND PEPPER TO TASTE

3 TABLESPOONS CHILI POWDER

1 TABLESPOON CUMIN

1 CUP GUACAMOLE

   LARGE TOOTHPICKS, FOR SPEARING THE CARNITAS

   FRESH CILANTRO, LIME WEDGES, AND/OR SALSA FOR GARNISH (OPTIONAL)

Cut the pork into 1½-inch cubes. Place the pork cubes on a shallow, lightly greased baking pan. Sprinkle with salt, pepper, chili powder, and cumin. Bake in a 325° oven for 1 hour. Stir now and then, draining excess fat. To serve, drain and place on a warmed platter with guacamole and/or salsa. Eat carnitas using toothpicks.

This will serve 4.

For this dish, you want a cut of pork that has a little fat to produce crispy carnitas.

HOT/WARM

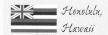

Honolulu, Hawaii

Teriyaki Beef Sticks

When I stay in Honolulu, one of the first places I always want to visit is the House Without a Key. This is an open-air café at the Halekulani Hotel. I like to arrive at sunset, when superb local musicians perform island tunes and Miss Hawaii often does the hula dance. The menu has many tempting appetizers, and one of my favorites is the beef teriyaki sticks. Teriyaki is a vital part of the food scene all over Honolulu. It is of Japanese origin: *teri* is "charcoal," and *yaki* means "broil." At this café overlooking the Pacific, the sticks are served on a bed of radiccio. Here is my version of this Hawaiian culinary delight.

One of the popular tourist food attractions in Honolulu is the diverse markets in Chinatown. They are filled with freshly roasted ducks, island watercress, local tropical fish, and small cafés. You can take a guided tour of this legendary section of Honolulu.

2   POUNDS TOP SIRLOIN OR FLANK STEAK
¼   CUP SOY SAUCE
2   TABLESPOONS SHERRY OR SAKE
1   TABLESPOON CRUSHED FRESH GINGER
1   CLOVE GARLIC, MINCED
2   TABLESPOONS BROWN SUGAR
2   TABLESPOONS SESAME OIL
    LIME SLICES AND CILANTRO FOR GARNISH (OPTIONAL)
8   BAMBOO SKEWERS, SOAKED IN WATER FOR 20 MINUTES TO
      PREVENT BURNING

Cut the steak in small, bite-sized pieces (about 40). Place in a flat, shallow dish. In a small bowl, combine remaining ingredients except garnishes and skewers (obviously), and pour sauce over meat, stirring so all meat is coated. Marinate in refrigerator 4 hours or overnight.

To cook, remove meat from sauce. Place 5 steak pieces on each skewer. Dribble remaining sauce over meat. Place under a broiler, or grill. Cook to desired doneness, turning once. Garnish with lime slices and cilantro if desired.

This will serve 8.

HOT/WARM

Honolulu Spareribs

Honolulu,
Hawaii

In Honolulu, spareribs in a shiny, tangy sauce are a traditional part of the *pupu* (Hawaiian for "appetizers") plate. Baby back ribs may be used, or ask your butcher to slice regular ribs into 2-inch lengths for you.

- ¼ CUP SOY SAUCE
- 2 TABLESPOONS BROWN SUGAR
- 2 TABLESPOONS SHERRY
- 1 TABLESPOON FRESH MINCED GINGER
- ½ CUP KETCHUP OR CHILI SAUCE
- 2 POUNDS SPARERIBS (BABY BACK, OR REGULAR CUT IN 2-INCH LENGTHS)
  CILANTRO LEAVES FOR GARNISH

Place ribs in flat, shallow baking pan. Set aside. In medium bowl, combine soy sauce, brown sugar, sherry, ginger, and ketchup or chili sauce. Pour over the ribs. Marinate the ribs in the sauce for at least an hour or even overnight. Bake for 1 hour in a 325° oven, turning once. These ribs may be placed under the broiler for added crispness at the last minute if desired. Garnish with cilantro.

Serves 6 to 8.

This is usually eaten with fingers. Be sure to provide napkins.

HOT/WARM

A Meatball Medley

Bite-sized meatballs have long been a tradition for the appetizer menu. They may be kept warm on a heat tray, candle warmer, or chafing dish. Of course, meatballs may be easily prepared ahead and reheated at your convenience. Provide toothpicks for spearing, and make sure there are napkins and little plates (paper is fine).

Stockholm Meatballs

 Stockholm, Sweden

Swedish meatballs are traditional for the hot appetizer menu. This recipe from the capital city is especially flavorful. You can ask your favorite butcher to grind the meat fresh for you.

- 2 TABLESPOONS BUTTER
- 1 MEDIUM ONION, FINELY CHOPPED
- 1 EGG, BEATEN
- ½ CUP MILK
- 1 CUP WHITE BREAD PIECES (CRUSTS REMOVED, 2 TO 3 SLICES)
- ½ POUND LEAN GROUND PORK
- ½ POUND GROUND VEAL
- ½ POUND LEAN GROUND BEEF
- SALT AND PEPPER TO TASTE
- ½ TEASPOON NUTMEG
- 2 TABLESPOONS BUTTER + 1 TABLESPOON VEGETABLE OIL FOR FRYING MEATBALLS
- 2 TABLESPOONS FLOUR + 1½ CUPS HALF AND HALF FOR GRAVY
- SALT AND PEPPER TO TASTE
- FRESH SNIPPED DILL OR PARSLEY FOR GARNISH

HOT/WARM

Melt 2 tablespoons of butter in a nonstick or other frying pan. Fry the onion just until limp and set aside. Mix the egg and milk in a small bowl. Place the bread in this mixture for 10 minutes to soften. In a large bowl, combine the meat, seasonings, and onion. The mixture should be smooth like a paste. The best way to achieve this is to use your hands to blend the mixture. This may be done ahead and refrigerated.

In a 10- to 12-inch frying pan (the original onion pan may be used—just be sure to remove any onion specks), heat butter and oil until hot but not smoking. Form the meat into balls about the size of walnuts. Fry over a medium flame, turning and shaking the pan so that the meatballs are brown on all sides. This will take around 10 minutes. Remove meatballs from pan, and drain on paper towels. With heat still on medium, add flour to pan, and stir to gather up drippings. Slowly add the half and half, with salt and pepper to taste. Blend and cook over low heat for 5 minutes. Place meatballs in a warmed dish. Pour gravy on top. Garnish with a few sprigs of fresh dill or parsley.

This will make around 24 meatballs.

Experiencing a smörgåsbord in Stockholm is a culinary treat. There will be a large buffet table filled with appetizing platters of cold and hot dishes (of which meatballs are a part). Ice-cold Aquavit is the traditional beverage.

Greece

Greek Meatballs
(Keftedakia)

This main-dish meatball is often made into an *orektika* (Greek for "appetizer") offering. The typically Greek flavorings of mint and cinnamon, combined with the cucumber-yogurt dip, give this dish a characteristic Greek spirit.

1   EGG, BEATEN
½   CUP SOFT BREAD PIECES (ABOUT 1 SLICE, CRUSTS REMOVED)
1   POUND LEAN GROUND BEEF (½ MAY BE GROUND LAMB)
1   GARLIC CLOVE, PEELED AND MINCED
1   SMALL ONION, FINELY CHOPPED (ABOUT ⅓ CUP)
1   TABLESPOON FINELY SNIPPED FRESH MINT
½   TEASPOON CINNAMON
    SALT AND PEPPER TO TASTE
¼   TO ½ CUP OLIVE OIL FOR FRYING
    ABOUT ½ CUP FLOUR FOR COATING

Dipping Sauce

½   CUP SHREDDED CUCUMBER
½   CUP PLAIN YOGURT
    SALT AND PEPPER TO TASTE
    MINT LEAVES OR CUCUMBER SLICES FOR GARNISH

Combine egg and bread pieces in large bowl; let bread pieces absorb egg for 15 minutes. Add remaining ingredients through salt and pepper, and mix well until blended. Dampen your hands with water, and make meatballs about the size of a large walnut.

Heat olive oil in a frying pan (nonstick will work well). You need only enough olive oil to prevent sticking. Lay flour out on a piece of waxed paper. Roll balls in the flour to coat. Fry meatballs

For the best-quality ground meat, select the cuts yourself. Then ask your local butcher to grind the meats for you. You can then be assured of the quality and freshness of your meat mixture. Remember, butchers do enjoy keeping their customers happy by offering their expertise.

HOT/WARM

until browned and cooked inside (about 10 minutes). Roll around in pan for even cooking. Remove and drain on paper towels.

Squeeze excess moisture from cucumber and combine with yogurt, salt, and pepper in a pretty bowl. Place warm meatballs on a platter with the yogurt-cucumber dip. Garnish with mint or some cucumber slices if desired. These are best served warm; however, they are also nice cool. Serve with pita bread or crackers.

This will serve 4 to 6.

Rome, Italy

Roman Meat Cakes
(Polpette)

When I lived in Rome, we would often visit the historic Trastevere neighborhood to dine. It is there that I first tasted these flavorful morsels, in a rustic trattoria. This recipe comes from the chef's sister. The appealing plate was garnished with lemon slices and parsley sprigs. This recipe may be made ahead and kept refrigerated until needed.

1   EGG
1   SLICE WHITE BREAD
¼   CUP RED OR WHITE WINE
1   POUND LEAN GROUND BEEF
2   TEASPOONS MINCED PARSLEY
    SALT AND PEPPER TO TASTE
    PINCH NUTMEG
1   CLOVE GARLIC, MINCED
    RIND OF 1 MEDIUM LEMON, GRATED
    OLIVE OIL FOR FRYING
    LEMON WEDGES AND PARSLEY SPRIGS FOR GARNISH

Lightly beat the egg in a medium-sized bowl. Crumble in the bread and bread crust, and add wine. Let stand a few minutes for the wine to absorb. Add remaining ingredients through lemon rind, and mix together.

Form the mixture into flat cakes about ⅓ inch high and 1½ inches in diameter. Heat enough olive oil in a nonstick or other frying pan to make an even layer about ¼ inch deep. Fry the cakes on each side until golden brown. Garnish with lemon wedges and parsley sprigs, and serve.

This will make about 20 cakes.

Traditionally, these meat cakes are served warm, but they are also quite tasty when cool.

HOT/WARM

Asian Meatballs

 China

This combination of Pacific-Asian flavors is seductive and always mouth-wateringly delicious.

1   POUND LEAN GROUND PORK (HAVE YOUR BUTCHER GRIND THIS FRESHLY)

1   EGG, BEATEN

½   CUP COARSELY CHOPPED WATER CHESTNUTS

1   TABLESPOON FRESHLY MINCED GINGER

1   GARLIC CLOVE, PEELED AND MINCED

2   TABLESPOONS CORNSTARCH

1   TABLESPOON SESAME OIL

1   TABLESPOON SOY SAUCE

½   TEASPOON SALT

    FRESHLY GROUND PEPPER TO TASTE

1   TABLESPOON SESAME OIL FOR FRYING

1   TABLESPOON VEGETABLE OR PEANUT OIL FOR FRYING

    CILANTRO LEAVES FOR GARNISH

These can also be served with a dipping sauce of 1 cup soy sauce combined with 1 teaspoon dried or bottled mustard.

Combine meat, egg, water chestnuts, ginger, garlic, cornstarch, sesame, soy, salt, and pepper in a bowl. Form into little round balls, about 1½ inches in diameter. Heat oils in a nonstick frying pan, and fry meatballs on both sides until brown and cooked. Serve garnished with cilantro leaves.

This will serve 10 to 12.

HOT/WARM

Index